CW01475574

TOP DATING TIPS FOR WOMEN
&
INSTANT SPARK

2 Books in 1

EXPERT TIPS FOR IMPROVING YOUR LOVE LIFE
AND GETTING A PARTNER

SONIA WOOD

TOP DATING TIPS FOR WOMEN

SONIA WOOD

4

Disclaimer

This Book has been written for information purposes only. Every effort has been made to make this Book as complete and accurate as possible.

However, there may be mistakes in typography or content. Also, this Book provides information only up to the publishing date. Therefore, these Books should be used as a guide - not as the ultimate source.

The purpose of this Books is to educate. The author and the publisher do not warrant that the information contained in this Book is fully complete and shall not be responsible for any errors or omissions. The author and publisher shall have neither liability nor responsibility to any person or entity concerning any loss or damage caused or alleged to be caused directly or indirectly by this Book.

TABLE OF CONTENTS

INTRODUCTION

Are you looking at venturing into the dating scene, but don't know where to start? Or perhaps you're already on the market, but you're not having much luck at finding quality relationships.

Every single woman knows that finding the perfect match isn't easy regardless of how much dating experience you may have, or how many dating apps and websites you're on.

Even those exploring the dating scene with an open heart and mind are often quickly overwhelmed by the lack of interest in commitment or long-term relationships. It can feel as though like-minded individuals with the same goals and aspirations just aren't out there.

It can quickly become exhausting, both emotionally and mentally.

Worse, with so many dating websites and apps that connect singles at the click of a mouse, women are often finding themselves having to compete for attention in ways they never thought they would ever have to.

But it doesn't have to be so difficult.

Great dates that lead to long-term, life-changing relationships are within your reach when you prepare and equip yourself with a few simple strategies that will improve the quality of your dates and set you on the path towards finding that happily ever after.

In the next few chapters, we'll look at the top 10 dating tips that will boost the quality of your dates and help you find the perfect partner.

So, without further delay, let's begin!

TIP #1: SET THE SCENE

Where you look for the perfect partner is equally as important as how you look. In other words, set the scene so that you're putting yourself in the right line of sight.

Looking for potential mates in bars and clubs isn't exactly getting the odds on your side. Dating is hard enough let alone when you factor in trying to get to know someone on any sort of real level while downing shots or trying to talk over loud music and distractions.

Instead, consider the places where you can connect with someone and focus on planning dates in those relationship-nurturing settings. Save the bars for your girls' nights!

That being said, there is nothing wrong with spending a third or fourth date at a bar or club where you can dance and let your hair down, but it isn't usually recommended for your first or second date.

Those initial dates are the time to be focused on really getting to know one another and whether you're compatible so you're not wasting time and energy working on a relationship that isn't likely to go anywhere.

It's also when you get to explore interests, share hopes and dreams, and ensure that your future visions align.

You deserve that.

TIP #2: LOOK AROUND YOU

Many of us tend to overlook some of the greatest potential partners that are already part of our lives simply because we're too busy searching for something more.

In truth, some of the greatest love stories of all time began as friends.

Do you have someone in the friend zone who may be a potential love interest?

Have you connected with someone on a level that you haven't found with anyone else but perhaps you've never considered anything beyond the friendship you have?

You might be surprised that your perfect partner is already part of your life.

Makes sense, right?

Your friends already know you. They likely share the same interests, passions, values, and aspirations.

If that's the case, half the work of the initial dating process is behind you. You've already spent time connecting, you've let your guard down and you've likely shared more with them than you would with someone you've just started dating.

Does anyone come to mind? If so, maybe it's time to explore the possibilities.

TIP #3: CONNECT TO LOVE

Dating sites can certainly make life easier when it comes to seeing what's out there, testing the waters, and connecting with a wide range of people in a short amount of time.

But not all dating sites are created equal and it's important that you carefully consider the sites and networks you choose so that you're maximizing the time spent searching for a partner.

Dating sites that are designed to connect specific age groups or other demographics will help you increase your chances of finding someone compatible, rather than signing up for sites where potential partners are looking for someone entirely different.

Choosing the right dating site is also important because it decreases the chances of you ending up disappointed or feeling hopeless because you haven't been able to find matches or get anywhere beyond an initial introduction.

The type of site you choose will depend on what is most important to you, as well as your age, location, and gender, but they often go beyond that.

Consider dating sites that focus on specific lifestyles.

This may include:

- Career based dating sites such as the military.

- Religion-based dating sites.

- 40+ dating sites.

- Location-based dating sites.

- Education-based dating sites.

- Divorcees or Widow based dating sites.

The more focused the dating site is on what is most in line with your lifestyle, the easier it will be to find great matches.

Here are a few dating sites with a specific focus on connecting people who share similar lifestyles:

https://www.PassionsNetwork.com

https://www.CoffeeMeetsBagel.com

https://www.ChristianCafe.com

https://www.ChristianMingle.com

https://www.JDate.com

https://www.Zoosk.com

https://dating.silversingles.com

TIP #4: LET YOUR GUARD DOWN

For years, women have been told that men love a good chase and that overly aggressive women aren't likely to find someone that will take them seriously.

Forget everything you've ever heard because, in today's world, the playing field has been leveled.

Men love being chased just as much as women do and, in many cases,, men will feel far more at ease with a woman who isn't afraid of showing him that she's interested.

Imagine how much easier it will be to get to know someone you're attracted to if they know they're not wasting their time and that you're serious about connecting with them on a deeper level.

Playing coy isn't always the best strategy when it comes to great dates that lead to everlasting relationships. Playing "hard to get" could make you come across as cold, distant, and disinterested. It could also make him feel uncomfortable and create an awkward vibe that just doesn't need to be there.

So, if you're interested in him, don't be afraid to show it. Nurture the conversation with body language that lets him know you're genuinely interested in him.

Sure, if he cracks a joke that you don't funny, you don't have to laugh. You don't want to come across as phony! That's not your style, right?

Instead, don't be afraid to banter, to show off your sense of humor and tease each other affectionately. It's a great way to break down those walls and get over the nervousness that comes from new relationships.

TIP #5: BECOME AN ATTENTIVE LISTENER

Oversharing happens to the best of us. We get nervous and feel awkward and suddenly we're dealing with a serious case of word vomit.

It's easy to lead the conversation to a point where we're not tuned in to what someone else is trying to say, so it's important to make sure you're listening just as much as you're sharing.

You also should take your time answering questions that he may have for you. Not only will your responses be more thoughtful and genuine, but if you aren't too quick to blurt something out, you'll be able to avoid saying something you regret.

Plus, becoming an attentive listener is a great way to let him know that you're truly interested in getting to know him. The more questions you ask, and the more often you direct conversations away from talking too much about yourself, the easier the conversation will flow.

At the same time, you want to be careful not to fire a dozen questions at him too quickly. Make sure he's comfortable answering questions and avoid going anywhere near the too-personal zone until you've had a chance to get to know each other and are aware of one another's comfort zones.

Instead, keep the conversation focused on interests, hobbies, and passions. Avoid talking about past relationships; at least in the beginning.

Those deeper conversations can happen later once you've gotten off on the right foot and you've determined there's a level of compatibility worthy of another date.

TIP #6: PAY ATTENTION TO BODY LANGUAGE

Body language speaks louder than words ever could. If you want to know what he's feeling, and whether he's genuinely interested in getting to know beyond sexual attraction, you'll want to pay close attention to where his gaze rests and whether he leans in when he speaks to you.

Research has shown that when someone is truly attracted to another, they often allow their gaze to linger on the person's face that they're talking to, rather than scan their body.

And remember, this goes both ways.

Your body language will tell your date whether you're interested in him or not so if you want to show him, you're attracted, let your body language tell the story.

Here are a few tips!

Make Eye Contact:

Not only is this a sign of respect, but it tells him that you're interested in what he has to say.

Posture:

Your posture can indicate that you're tired or bored just as much as it can tell him you're feeling a connection. Slouching indicates a lack of energy and interest so sit up straight or lean in his direction.

Smile!

It's the easiest way to let someone know you're interested in them and it's simply a universal sign of happiness. It's also a great way to flirt without going overboard.

Let your body language represent your interest or connection in someone and boost the quality of your dates up by making it clear that you're having a great time and are thoroughly enjoying your time together.

TIP #7: LISTEN TO YOUR INSTINCTS

It's easy to get excited about a date and share your experiences with friends and family to get feedback or validation that there might be something worthy of perusing.

The problem comes when you end up misadvised, or you follow the advice from someone who may not have your best interests at heart.

Or perhaps they simply don't know the person you're dating and are basing their opinions on their past dating failures or expectations.

You must follow your instincts (and heart!) when it comes to dating. If the person makes you feel comfortable and you are finding yourself having a great time, don't let anyone discourage you from seeing it through.

You know yourself better than anyone, and so if you pay attention to what your gut is telling you, and you go into every date with an open heart and mind, you'll never be misled.

TIP #8: PUT YOURSELF FIRST

A lot of us are fearful of hurting someone's feelings, especially when it comes to rejection.

The truth is, you owe it to yourself to value your time and energy and so if you aren't feeling a connection, don't let someone else's feelings, or your concern that he'll be discouraged, get in the way of your feelings.

Always do what's best for yourself first.

Let him down gently, but firmly. You are looking for love and every date you go out on takes up a lot of mental and emotional energy so you need to keep those tanks filled.

Wasting time on dates that you know aren't going to lead anywhere are not only robbing you of finding true love, but it's also not fair to the person you're spending time with.

It's easy to lead someone on out of fear of causing them pain but in the end, he will respect your honesty because it sets him free so he can continue his journey to find his perfect match. Don't play games.

TIP #9: DON'T OVER-RESEARCH

While it's important to take measures to ensure your safety when going out on dates, you don't want to do so much research that there's little left to learn about someone you're potentially interested in.

Over-researching can also lead to pre-judging. Don't end up with a tainted viewpoint simply because you've uncovered bits and pieces about someone without knowing his entire story.

Give him a fair chance! Unless you've uncovered things about him that cause you to feel genuinely concerned, or may put your safety in harm's way, leave it up for discovery as you get to know him. A little mystery can add a lot of excitement to a new relationship.

And finally, don't ask your friends to tell you everything they know about him! If you're being set up by a friend, trust their judgment and leave it at that.

Learn for yourself how you feel about him and let the magic happen organically.

TIP #10: KEEP IT IN PRESENT

We've discussed the damage to what could have been a potentially genuine connection by over-sharing and it's especially true when it comes to discussing your past relationships.

Even if your previous relationship ended on good terms you don't want to involve him in your conversation.

So, no saying things like, "you look just like my ex!". Not only is comparing him to someone from your past disrespectful, but it will just make things awkward.

No one wants to feel like they'll need to compete with someone's past, so don't put that on him.

Plus, if you tend to talk about your ex, chances are you're not over him which will be a huge red flag to a potential new partner.

FINAL WORDS

So, there you have it! We've covered the top 10 tips to improving the quality of your dates and setting yourself on the path towards making and nurturing genuine connections.

Now it's up to you. You deserve to be happy and to find a partner that makes you feel as though you're the only woman on earth, but how you go about it will make or break your chances at finding that special someone.

I hope these tips and strategies help you find love. To further help you on your journey I'm including links to websites dedicated to providing additional tips from dating experts as well as some other useful resources.

Here's to your finding you're happily ever after!

RESOURCES

Here are links to a few resources to help you continue your journey to finding everlasting love:

Dating Websites:

https://www.PassionsNetwork.com

https://www.CoffeeMeetsBagel.com

https://www.ChristianCafe.com

https://www.ChristianMingle.com

https://www.JDate.com

https://www.Zoosk.com

https://dating.silversingles.com/

Expert Dating Tips:

https://www.catchhimandkeephim.com/dating/

Dating Coaching & Online Classes:

https://theartofcharm.com/

INSTANT SPARK

SONIA WOOD

Disclaimer

This Book has been written for information purposes only. Every effort has been made to make this Book as complete and accurate as possible.

However, there may be mistakes in typography or content. Also, this Book provides information only up to the publishing date. Therefore, these Books should be used as a guide - not as the ultimate source.

The purpose of this Books is to educate. The author and the publisher do not warrant that the information contained in this Book is fully complete and shall not be responsible for any errors or omissions. The author and publisher shall have neither liability nor responsibility to any person or entity concerning any loss or damage caused or alleged to be caused directly or indirectly by this Book.

INTRODUCTION

Are you looking to up your dating game and learn how to attract the right kind of women? Interested in mastering the art of seduction and learning how to engage dates in meaningful conversation while leaving a positive impression?

Whether you have a crush on someone or you're just venturing into the world of dating, there are proven ways to maximize your chances of finding love.

This special report is dedicated to just that: helping you avoid dates that crash and burn so you can find that special someone who is meant for you.

So, without further delay, let's get started!

THE ART OF ENGAGEMENT

It's easy to get excited when meeting someone we see as a potential partner and wanting to spill everything.

So, we end up oversharing... and then what happens?

She ends up sitting there listening to you talking incessantly about yourself, all the while you believe you're simply lowering your guard and doing your best to engage, she's either bored, annoyed, or both.

We've all done it so don't feel bad if you identify with this scenario. Sometimes we catch it early enough to back-track and do damage control by reverting the conversation to her so we can show her that we're truly interested.

Other times, we fail to recognize how we're dominating the conversation and the date ends with little chance of ever hearing from her again. It's like a job interview. Blow it and it's over.

Learning to communicate takes work. It's not something we're all naturally gifted with. Sure, we know how to ask all the right questions and we certainly know how to talk about ourselves but a deep conversation that leaves both people feeling satisfied isn't always as easy as we may think.

The key is to listen just as much as we share.

Yeah, I know. You've probably been told that you should simply do all the listening, but the truth is a great conversation is about both of you putting in an equal effort. It's a give and takes an exchange where each person is truly invested in getting to know one another. It's never one-sided.

You want to share the spotlight so you can be sure she feels that you're genuinely interested in everything she has to say, rather than throwing out a round of rapid-fire questions only because you think you're expected to do so.

Because nothing turns a woman off more than a disengaged man who is wrapped up in conversational narcissism.

Leaving a positive impression where she thinks of you long after the date ends comes down to being authentic and charming. And believe me, any man can learn these skills.

Here are a few tips that will help you master the art of conversation and leave her wanting more:

Avoid Boring, Stock Questions

Asking "What do you do for fun?" isn't just uncreative but it's flat-out boring. Those kinds of questions won't leave her captivated or even remotely engaged. They lack thought and quite simply, they feel scripted.

Sure, you can use these traditional questions as a starting point, but they need to be designed so they lead to more in-depth, engaging questions. The initial stock question should give you the chance to press further so that follow-up questions are more thought-provoking.

Just remember, you never want to feel as though you're interrogating her. Share as much as she is. Match her pace and comfort level. And tailor the conversation to her rather than making the mistake of following a one-strategy-fits-all approach.

Example:

A standard question might be "Where did you grow up?", and then a far more thought-provoking follow-up question could be, "Does that place still feel like home to you?" or "What was your favorite thing about living there?"

Lead with a Compliment

Don't listen to anyone who tells you that leading with a compliment is lame or cheesy. If it's a genuine compliment, rooted in truth, it'll make her feel good about herself and simultaneously help her lower her guard and feel comfortable.

Avoid anything sexual. You want to compliment her in a way that doesn't sexualize her in any way, especially if it's your first date. Sexy, flirty compliments will come later. For now, start by showing her you're paying attention by complimenting her in a way that not only disarms her but leaves her wanting more.

Come Armed & Ready

Before your next date, think about the type of questions you could ask her. Brainstorm stories you can share and think about the types of topics she is likely interested in. Even if you don't know much about her, there are tried & true topics that will peak nearly everyone's interest.

Just avoid the obvious triggers: income, sex, politics, and religion.

Go Deep

We're all guilty of engaging in surface-conversation. Small talk and discussions that barely graze the depths of anything deeply fulfilling. It's easy to ask her how she likes her job, right? There's one of those stock questions you want to avoid. Instead, ask her what her greatest challenges are in her career, or what she feels will change in her chosen profession.

Dig deeper but do so carefully. Don't pry if you get the impression that she's not comfortable talking in great depth about certain topics.

At the same time, by engaging her in conversation that goes beyond the formalities of casual banter, you're demonstrating a real interest in getting to know who she is and what makes her tick.

Take Your Time

Well, thought out responses and questions will go the distance so slow things down and think before you speak.

Most foot-in-mouth moments happen because we're too busy responding without being thoughtful. You can easily avoid this by pausing briefly so you can collect your thoughts and give her a genuine answer to her questions that you won't later regret.

HOW TO AVOID THE FRIEND ZONE

Do nice guys finish last?

There's one place that no man wants to find themselves in and that's the dreaded friend zone.

What begins as a potential relationship where you are investing the time and energy into getting to know her, suddenly shifts into some strange, awkward, and then way-too-comfortable space where she stops looking at you as a possible love interest and begins to see you as a good, trusted friend.

If you've ever experienced this before then you know how hard it can be to change gears and get back into the romantic partner category once she sees you as a buddy.

So, you need to arm yourself with the tools needed to ensure you never get placed into the friend zone.

Here's how to get started:

Stop Hanging Out and Start Dating

The truth is, whether you end up in the friend zone or not isn't always within your control, however, there is one thing you can do to set the stage so that your chances of that happening are seriously minimized.

It requires that you stop "hanging out" with the women you're interested in and you start dating them.

Dating involves two people with a potential love interest. You are in a temporarily committed relationship that involves getting to know each other to determine whether you're romantically compatible.

But there's a fine line between dating and just hanging out and you need to be very careful not to fall into the wrong category, otherwise, you'll likely find yourself in the friend zone. And friend zone is nothing short of a lack of sexual interest.

Dating = Pathway to finding romance.

Hanging out = Pathway to becoming friends.

This means every date must have a purpose. For example, you're not just taking her to a hockey game because you both share a mutual interest in watching the sport.

Sure, the shared interest is great, but it should be the **foundation** of the date (the setting), not the **purpose** (to find love).

The purpose is to spend time together as a potential couple. It's seeing how you both interact and engage with one another, how you feel spending a few hours in different settings and situations. It's about testing the waters of romance.

So, during that date to the hockey game, consider the different ways you can set the tone so that she knows you are interested in her as more than friends.

Be romantic, be sweet, and above all, be genuine and nurturing. Engage in conversation that goes beyond surface chatter (read the previous chapter if you need help with that), and always stay focused on the real purpose of the date.

Here are a few tips to keep yourself out of the friend zone:

Be Playful and Flirty

Don't be afraid to flirt with her. This banter stage of dating is important because it clarifies your intentions and tells her that you are interested in her, well beyond just friends.

Keep it light, joking, and playful.

Don't be Subtle

Don't play hard to get or hold back when feeling the attraction. Men who find themselves in the friend zone are often there because they didn't make their interest known and instead were subtle flirters.

If you're worried about coming off too strong, think about the alternative: that you make her feel you just aren't interested enough. If you need to turn it down, she'll let you know.

Build Sexual Tension

As just mentioned, flirting is important because it shows interest in a sexual way, but you want to do your best to work on building sexual tension as well.

You can do this through playful, lingering touching such as placing her hand on her shoulder, or her lower back when guiding her through the crowd.

Women love the possessive touch of a man they're interested in because it makes them feel special and desired.

Don't Talk Yourself Down

Guys who end up in the friend zone are notorious for putting themselves down to lighten conversations or to simply come off as humble.

The truth is men who constantly self-deprecate aren't sexy. Sure, you might get a laugh or two and think that you're being endearing, but when it comes to relationships, you want her thinking of you sexually, not as a stand-up comedian who highlights all the reasons, she shouldn't be attracted to you.

Intense Goodbyes

If the date ends on a high note, let her know that you're hesitant to end it even though you need to. Leave her wanting more and always end the date while the excitement and energy are at an all-time high.

It'll take some experience to know when the timing is right, so keep a pulse on how the conversation is flowing and whether things are moving along or it's a good time to end the date.

HOT DATE IDEAS

The perfect date begins with the perfect setting. Get this wrong and you've made things so much harder on yourself.

When it comes to choosing the right setting, there are a few things to keep in mind, including:

A Setting that Promotes Intimate Conversations

This means you want to avoid rowdy bars with loud music that makes it impossible to hear one another. Instead, choose places that nurture conversation and allow you to both relax and get to know one another.

A Setting That's Affordable

Whether you can afford it or not isn't the point. Bringing her to expensive restaurants may send a signal of high expectations and create a tense and awkward interaction. Instead, choose casual places that set a comfortable tone, free of strings attached.

A Setting That's Interesting

Go off the beaten path and do something fun and interesting. Rather than the cliché walk on the beach, consider going hiking, ice skating, or kayaking.

Not only will you show her you're putting thought into the date but you'll build memories and have stories to share.

Okay, so we know the top 3 things to consider when choosing the right setting for a date. Need a few ideas? Here are our top 3 hot date spots:

Museum

It's not only an interesting way to spend some time together but there will be no shortage of topics to discuss as you move through different areas of the museum and explore together. It's also extremely affordable and allows you to spend as much (or as little) time together as you want without pressure.

Picnic

This never goes out of style. A well-thought-out picnic can set the stage for a memorable date. Plus, you can tailor the picnic based on whether it's a first date, third date, or a tenth date!

For example, keep things casual and light if it's the first date. For a second date? Pack a bottle of wine! For a later date, consider adding more romance to the setting.

Coffee Shop

There's no better place to have a real conversation, free from distractions, than a casual coffee shop. There's no pressure, they're usually rather quiet and you can start here and see where it goes.

THE ART OF SEDUCTION

So, we've discussed the ways of staying clear from the friend zone and we've gone over the art of conversation. Now it's time to think about another important part of every high-intensity romance: mastering the **art of seduction.**

Seduction is all about the long game. You'll need to invest the time and energy into utilizing every skillset in your arsenal, including humor, wit, and charm.

It's also about being attentive but not coming off as cheesy or desperate. And sometimes, it's about "faking it till you make it", especially when it comes to conveying confidence.

You might not feel like you're the best catch out there. You may question yourself at every turn or wonder why she's into you. You'll need to learn to move beyond all self-doubt because one of the biggest romance-killers is insecurity.

Instead, you'll want to work on charm and sophistication. You'll win her over easily when you present yourself as someone more than worthy: you're irresistible.

Here's how:

1: Dress the Part

A well-groomed man is attractive to women. Not only does it show her that you take care of yourself, but it also tells her that you put effort into looking your best for her.

You want to dress smartly and learn what kind of clothing suits your frame. Don't choose anything too loud. You want to highlight your masculinity while looking trendy.

2: Slow & Steady Wins the Race

When it comes to the art of seduction, it's all about taking your time with the woman of your dreams. Go slow, be thoughtful, and caring. A woman wants to feel protected and safe.

Even the most independent women on earth want to know that their man will take care of them so be aware of how she's feeling and make sure she's always comfortable.

3: Give her your full attention

Confident men know that to play hard to get is a game left for amateurs. Instead, shower her with attention so she feels respected and needed.

Flirt with her, be playful, and make her feel as though she's the only woman in the world. Never, ever pay another woman more attention to date.

The objective is to make her feel so special that all her insecurities are tossed aside.

4: Be Romantic

Create the perfect date by choosing the right setting. Go the extra mile. For example, if you are taking her out for dinner consider choosing an intimate table at a bistro and order a bottle of her favorite wine.

Avoid the loud, bustling bar scene and instead focus on settings that allow you to get to know one another.

5: Be Attentive

You need to make sure you are truly listening to what she is willing to share with you. Ask questions, go beyond surface conversation (I know, I've mentioned this already but it's incredibly important).

Don't come off too strong with personal questions until you've learned what she is comfortable sharing but at the same time, don't be afraid to ask her things about herself that allow you to know what makes her tick.

6: Get Closer

Look for natural opportunities to get closer. Whether it's the chance to sit closer to her at dinner or to take her for a walk where you can hold her hand, you should always be on the lookout for the perfect chance to flirt and be playful.

FINAL WORDS

Finding that special someone takes time and effort. You need to commit to the long-game and understand that real love takes hard work but it'll certainly pay off in the end.

Don't beat yourself up over failed dates. The more you put yourself out there and the more experience you gain, the easier it will be to feel confident and comfortable on future dates.

The truth is: practice makes perfect when it comes to the art of dating.

Don't give up. Whether you're new to the dating scene or not, you have everything it takes to become a charming, attractive, and unforgettable date. Believe in yourself and that you are worthy because you are.

The key is to pay attention to the signals she puts out, work towards engaging in deep conversations that lead to forming a strong connection, and never be afraid to let her know how you feel.

You've got this, dude. Now go find the love of your life!

To your happiness.

RESOURCES

Here are links to a few resources that I believe will help you:

Good Men Project:

https://goodmenproject.com/category/sex-relationships/

A blog dedicated to all things personal development and news-worthy.

Love Panky:

https://www.lovepanky.com/

A website focusing on finding love and building ever-lasting bonds.

The Modern Man:

https://www.themodernman.com

Essential dating advice for men.

CPSIA information can be obtained
at www.ICGtesting.com
Printed in the USA
BVHW040742060221
599449BV00006B/80